IT'S TIME TO LEARN ABOUT BABOONS

It's Time to Learn about Baboons

Walter the Educator

Silent King Books
A WhichHead Entertainment Imprint

Copyright © 2025 by Walter the Educator

All rights reserved. No part of this book may be reproduced in any manner whatsoever without written per- mission except in the case of brief quotations embodied in critical articles and reviews.

First Printing, 2024

Disclaimer

This book is a literary work; the story is not about specific persons, locations, situations, and/or circumstances unless mentioned in a historical context. Any resemblance to real persons, locations, situations, and/or circumstances is coincidental. This book is for entertainment and informational purposes only. The author and publisher offer this information without warranties expressed or implied. No matter the grounds, neither the author nor the publisher will be accountable for any losses, injuries, or other damages caused by the reader's use of this book. The use of this book acknowledges an understanding and acceptance of this disclaimer.

It's Time to Learn about Baboons is a collectible early learning book by Walter the Educator suitable for all ages belonging to Walter the Educator's Time to Eat Book Series. Collect more books at WaltertheEducator.com

USE THE EXTRA SPACE TO TAKE NOTES AND DOCUMENT YOUR MEMORIES

BABOONS

Baboons are monkeys, big and strong,

It's Time to Learn about

Baboons

With furry coats and tails so long.

They love to run, they love to play,

In troops they travel every day.

Their faces bare, their noses wide,

With clever hands, they climb with pride.

They chatter, bark, and make a fuss,

To talk to friends, like me and us!

They live in lands so hot and dry,

On rocky hills and mountains high.

They search for food both near and far,

From roots to fruits, they know where they are!

With sharp, big teeth, they chew their treats,

Like nuts and bugs and yummy meats.

They share their meals, they groom with care,

To show their love, their bonds are rare.

It's Time to Learn about

Baboons

A troop of baboons stays so tight,

Together strong from dawn to night.

The leader watches, brave and bold,

Keeping young ones safe and told.

Their tails go up when they are glad,

But when afraid, they might look mad!

They warn the troop with cries so loud,

Then off they run, a fleeing crowd!

They leap through trees and climb up high,

With hands and feet, they touch the sky.

They jump on rocks and race so fast,

Like little flashes running past!

The baby baboons hold on tight,

To moms who hug them through the night.

They learn to play, they learn to run,

It's Time to Learn about

Baboons

Their world is wild and full of fun!

Though sometimes loud, though sometimes bold,

Baboons are smart, their stories told.

They use their minds to find what's best,

Solving puzzles, passing tests!

So if you see a baboon troop,

Watch them chatter, climb, and swoop.

They live in nature, free and true,

It's Time to Learn about

Baboons

And now you know them, through and through!

ABOUT THE CREATOR

Walter the Educator is one of the pseudonyms for Walter Anderson. Formally educated in Chemistry, Business, and Education, he is an educator, an author, a diverse entrepreneur, and he is the son of a disabled war veteran. "Walter the Educator" shares his time between educating and creating. He holds interests and owns several creative projects that entertain, enlighten, enhance, and educate, hoping to inspire and motivate you. Follow, find new works, and stay up to date with Walter the Educator™

at WaltertheEducator.com

www.ingramcontent.com/pod-product-compliance
Lightning Source LLC
LaVergne TN
LVHW052017060526
838201LV00059B/4070